Joanne,

Lo...
Ent.
Of
Delight with
You!

— Your Sven, op.

Love

ALSO BY JOHN TRAIN

Coup de foudre

Love

Considered by
Casanova, Mark Twain, Shakespeare,
Oscar Wilde, Sigmund Freud, Byron,
La Rochefoucauld, John Updike,
and many others

Compiled and Edited by
John Train
Illustrated by Pierre Le-Tan

HarperCollins*Publishers*

FIRST EDITION
Designed by Katy Homans
Typeset in Monotype Dante by Michael & Winifred Bixler

Library of Congress Cataloging-in-Publication Data
Love : considered by Casanova, Mark Twain, Shakespeare, Oscar Wilde, Sigmund Freud, Byron, La Rochefoucauld, John Updike and many others—compiled and edited by John Train.
    p. cm.
    Includes index.
    ISBN 0–06–018237–7
    1. Love—Literary collections. 2. Love—Humor.
    I. Train, John.
PN6071.L7L623   1993
808.8'0354—dc20   92–56206

93 94 95 96 97 CW 10 9 8 7 6 5 4 3 2 1

CONTENTS

For Francie

No peevish winter wind shall chill
No sullen tropic sun shall wither
The roses in the rose-garden which is ours
  and ours only.

T. S. Eliot, from *A Dedication to my Wife*

Yonder a maid and her wight
  Come whispering by:
War's annals will cloud into night
  Ere their story die.

—Thomas Hardy

ACKNOWLEDGMENTS

I am grateful to Stephanie Lovell-Smith for research, to Linda Kelly for suggestions, and to Sara Perkins for editorial assistance. Morton M. Hunt's *Natural History of Love*, an interesting book, furnished a number of leads.

INTRODUCTION

For the Greeks, love—*eros*—was a madness, so powerful a force that it had to be attributed to a god or
daimon. Aphrodite's hold on a man could explain any
act, even in a court of law. The elders on the walls of
Troy, contemplating Helen, found it not remarkable
that for her men would suffer so. Euripides says it thus:

> All life that is wild and young
> In mountain and wave and stream
> All that of earth is sprung
> Or breathes in the red sunbeam;
> Yea, and mankind: O'er all a royal throne
> Cyprian, Cyprian, is thine alone.*

I define love for our purpose as the passion of one
being for another in the hope of being loved in return.

Hippolitus, trans. Gilbert Murray. Although Cyprian Aphrodite
was the wife of lame Hephaestus, she loved many others, includ-
ing Hermes and Dionysus. She was bedded with Ares when her
husband came upon the pair and caught them in a golden net.
He then summoned the other gods to witness their shame. But
Hermes observed that he would willingly change places with
Ares then and there.

A passion for something that cannot reciprocate, such as money, power over others, is another matter altogether. Greed seems to stem from a deficiency of love. Love of country, patriotism, is a combination of the herd instinct—sometimes the strongest of all influences—and our ties to place and culture. Men will die for it, but patriotism is not *eros*.*

And divine love? To suppose that the First Cause behind the inconceivable explosion we call big bang has human emotions is impious, however much we intuit God in our own image. We should not assume that God loves a creature as creatures love each other. However, the nonerotic kind of human love, *agape*—"charity" in the King James version, or perhaps "compassion"—helps us apprehend the divine nature, whence Jalaluddin Rumi's noble insight, "The astrolabe of the mysteries of God is love." But God may not respond. We cannot here discuss the ecstatic states of the mystics: Love and illumination are their metaphors for transcendent rapture.

It is not surprising that the language of gallantry, as of cuisine and war, is often the courtly tongue of the

---

*Aphrodite and the other Olympians are, in a way, metaphors for the chemicals behind our passions. Thus we say "martial," "jovial," "saturnine," or "mercurial." Mars is a personification of adrenaline. Eros—"being in love" is associated with phenylethylamine. In mother love, the baby's cry awakens the mother's lactogenic hormone, which gives her sensations of tenderness.

Normans: Assignation, rendezvous, and affair come straight from French; *billet-doux, coup de foudre, belle laide, gage d'amour, amitié amoureuse, tête-à-tête, ménage à trois*, and *cinq-à-sept* do not even have neat English equivalents.*

J. T.

*Brief love note; sudden passion; nice-looking but not pretty woman (see p. 24, La Bruyère); handsome present, usually jewelry, offered by rich admirer; long, affectionate intimacy; being sweetly alone together; marriage with a regular mistress or lover in the picture; after-work assignation. "Bastard," by the way, comes from an old French word for "saddle"—i.e., the product of a traveler's casual coupling.

Love

HEAD OVER HEELS

Sally

Sally came out in the spring. When she left I'd walked a good way from the station before it hit me. I had to sit down on a bench. It was impossible to imagine how to get through the rest of the day without her. The sense of loss was overwhelming, physical: quite different from anything I'd experienced before. Every part of me hurt, I couldn't move, so I just sat there, amazed, frightened and somehow overjoyed that any emotion, even pain, could be so huge.

—P. J. Kavanagh, *The Perfect Stranger*

Coup de Foudre

Who ever loved that loved not at first sight?

—Christopher Marlowe, *Hero and Leander*

Molly

. . . yes when I put the rose in my hair like the Andalusian girls used or shall I wear a red yes and how he kissed me under the Moorish wall and I thought well as well him as another and then I asked him with my eyes to ask again yes and then he asked me would I yes to say yes my mountain flower and first I put my arms around him yes and drew him down to me so he could feel my breasts all perfume yes and his heart was going like mad and yes I said yes I will Yes.

—James Joyce, *Ulysses*

Close

Oh let me be as close to you
As the wet skirt of a salt girl
To her body.
I think of you all the time.

—Akahito, eighth century A.D.

Yearning

O Western wind, when wilt thou blow
That the small rain down can rain?
Christ, that my love were in my arms
And I in my bed again!

—Anon.

Ardor

Contemporaries describe how the young Duc and Duchesse of Chartres would excuse themselves from dinner to borrow the hosts' bed for a while.

Offering

I was at a party feeling very shy because there were a lot of celebrities around, and I was sitting in a corner alone and a very beautiful young man came up to me and offered me some salted peanuts and said "I wish they were emeralds" as he handed me the peanuts and that was the end of my heart. I never got it back.

—Helen Hayes

Symptoms

[He manifested] all Sappho's famous signs*—his voice faltered, his face flushed up, his eyes glanced stealthily, a sudden sweat broke out on his skin, the beatings of his heart were irregular and violent.

—Plutarch, *Life of Demetrius*

*"I sweat, I tremble. I turn pale as grass."

The Real Thing

But she was filled with a strange, wild, unfamiliar happiness, and knew that this was love. Twice in her life she had mistaken something else for it; it was like seeing somebody in the street who you think is a friend, you whistle and wave and run after him, and it is not only not the friend, but not even very like him. A few minutes later the real friend appears in view, and then you can't imagine how you ever mistook that other person for him. Linda was now looking upon the authentic face of love, and she knew it, but it frightened her. That it should come so casually, so much by a series of accidents, was frightening. She tried to remember how she had felt when she had first loved her two husbands. There must have been strong and impelling emotion; in both cases she had disrupted her own life, upset her parents and friends remorselessly, in order to marry them, but she could not recall it. Only she knew that never before, not even in dreams, and she was a great dreamer of love, had she felt anything remotely like this. She told herself, over and over again, that tomorrow she must go back to London, but she had no intention of going back, and she knew it.

—Nancy Mitford, *The Pursuit of Love*

Far Gone

"She feels it in the air—love, I mean—and she's going very fast. She's got most of the symptoms—is twittery and cross, doesn't eat, lies awake, and said 'John,' as you do, and then turned red as a poppy. Whatever shall we do?" said Jo, looking ready for any measures, however violent.

"Nothing but wait. Let her alone, be kind and patient, and Father's coming will settle everything," replied her mother.

—Louisa May Alcott, *Little Women*

Initiation

We don't believe in rheumatism and true love until after the first attack.

—Marie Ebner von Eschenbach

ATTRACTION

Sight and Sound

A man falls in love through his eyes, a woman through her ears.*

—Woodrow Wyatt

Humor I

Among those whom I like or admire, I can find no common denominator, but among those whom I love, I can: all of them make me laugh.

—W. H. Auden

Humor II

Nothing spoils a romance so much as a sense of humour in the woman.

—Oscar Wilde

*Notably Cyrano. *Vide* Shakespeare's: "Love looks not with the eyes, but with the mind." (*A Midsummer Night's Dream.*)

Humor III

Asked by a gentleman friend why women seemed not
to have a sense of humor, Mrs. Pat Campbell replied,
"God did it on purpose, so that we may love you men
instead of laughing at you."

Beauty I

My love in her attire doth show her wit,
  It doth so well become her;
For every season she hath dressings fit,
  For winter, spring and summer.

No beauty she doth miss
When all her robes are on;
But Beauty's self she is
When all her robes are gone.

—Anon.

Beauty II

Perhaps men who cannot love passionately are those
who feel the effect of beauty most keenly; at any rate
this is the strongest impression women can make
on them.

—Stendhal, *De l'Amour*

Beauty III

When a plain-looking woman is loved it can only be very passionately; for either her influence over her lover is irresistible, or she has secret charms more powerful than those of beauty.

—Jean de la Bruyère, *Of the Affections*

Then and Now

During the last fifty years or thereabouts we have come to believe that the basis of all love is sexual, and that therefore any and every love which does not issue in sexual satisfaction is warped in its nature and in its effects. But when Dante loved it was otherwise. The lover who had set his heart upon the unattainable suffered, no doubt, the usual bodily frustrations, but he was not haunted by a guilty sense of personal failure and social inadequacy. On the contrary, he was admired and commended.

—Dorothy L. Sayers

The Grand Passion

It was Rousseau who first started the cult of passion for passion's sake. Before his time, the great passions, such as that of Paris for Helen, of Dido for Aeneas, of Paolo and Francesca for one another, had been regarded as disastrous maladies rather than as enviable states of soul. Rousseau, followed by all the romantic poets of France and England, transformed the grand passion from what it had been in the Middle Ages—a demonic possession—into a social obligation, and promoted it from the rank of a disease to that of the only true and natural form of love.

—Aldous Huxley

Some People

Some people like sex more than others—
You seem to like it a lot.
There's nothing wrong with being innocent
     or high-minded.
But I'm glad you're not.

—Wendy Cope, *Making Cocoa for Kingsley Amis*

Sweet and Twenty

What is love? 'tis not hereafter;
Present mirth hath present laughter;
   What's to come is still unsure;
   In delay there lies no plenty:
Then come kiss me, sweet and twenty,
   Youth's a stuff will not endure.

—William Shakespeare

STAGES OF LOVE

Greeting the Hostess

I [Ulysses] fared onward to the house of Circe, and my
heart was clouded with care as I walked along. When I
got to the gates I stood there and called the goddess,
and as soon as she heard me she came down, opened
the door, and asked me to come in; so I followed her,
much troubled in my mind. She set me on a richly
decorated seat inlaid with silver. There was a footstool
also under my feet. She mixed a mess in a golden gob-
let for me to drink, but she drugged it, for she meant
me mischief. When she had given it me and I had
drunk it without its charming me, she struck me with
her wand. "There now," she cried, "be off to the pig-
stye, and make your lair with the rest of them."

But I rushed at her with my sword drawn as though
I would kill her, whereon she fell with a loud scream,
clasped my knees, and spoke piteously, saying, "Who
and whence are you? From what place and people have
you come? How can it be that my drugs have no power
to charm you? Never yet was any man able to stand so
much as a taste of the herb I gave you; you must be
spellproof; surely you can be none other than the bold
hero Ulysses, who Mercury always said would come
here one day with his ship while on his way home from

Troy. So be it then. Sheathe your sword and let us go to bed, that we may make friends and learn to trust each other."

And I answered, "Circe, how can you expect me to be friendly with you when you have just been turning all my men into pigs? . . . I shall not consent to go to bed with you unless you will first take your solemn oath to plot no further harm against me."

So she swore at once as I had told her, and when she had completed her oath then I went to bed with her.

—Homer, *The Odyssey* (trans. Samuel Butler)

Display

In nine cases out of ten, a woman had better show more affection than she feels.

—Jane Austen

Stages

A woman can become a man's friend only in the following stages—first as an acquaintance, next as a mistress, and only then as a friend.

—Anton Chekhov, *Uncle Vanya*

Roles

Wives are young men's mistresses, companions for middle age, and old men's nurses.

—Francis Bacon

Desire

In real love you want the other person's good. In romantic love you want the other person.

—Margaret Anderson, *The Fiery Fountains*

Novelty

What the bloom is to the fruit, the charm of novelty is to love. It imparts a lustre which is easily effaced and which never returns.

—François, Duc de la Rochefoucauld

Rules of Courtly Love

Love is a certain inborn suffering derived from the sight of and excessive meditation upon the beauty of the opposite sex, which causes each one to wish above all things the embraces of the other and by common desire to carry out all of love's precepts in the other's embrace.

Some Rules

II He who is not jealous cannot love.
VIII No one should be deprived of love
without the very best of reasons.
X Love is always a stranger
in the home of avarice.
XI It is not proper to love any woman whom
one would be ashamed to seek to marry.
XIII When made public love rarely endures.

—*The Art of Courtly Love*, Andreas Capellanus,
twelfth century, trans. J. J. Parry

Echoes

When they first began to make love, she had felt
through his motions the habitual responses his wife
must make; while locked in this strange man's embrace she struggled jealously against the outline of the
other woman. On her part she bore the impress of
Richard's sexual style, so that in the beginning four
contending persons seemed involved on the sofa or in
the sand.

—John Updike, *Marry Me*

Constancy

Friendship is constant in all other things
Save in the office and affairs of love.

—William Shakespeare

Sisterhood

Women who love the same man have a kind of bitter freemasonry.

—Max Beerbohm, *Zuleika Dobson*

Trust

When my love swears that she is made of truth,
I do believe her, though I know she lies. . . .
Oh, love's best habit is in seeming trust,
And age in love loves not to have years told.
Therefore I lie with her and she with me.
And in our faults by lies we flattered be.

—William Shakespeare

Virility

Up until 100 a man is still a man, if you know what I mean . . . but after that it's not the same.

—Ancient Turk to *Life* reporter studying longevity

Improvement

It's odd how a person always arouses admiration for his moral qualities among the relatives of another with whom he has sexual relations. Physical love, so unjustifiably decried, makes everyone show, down to the least detail, all he has of goodness and self-sacrifice, so that he shines even in the eyes of those nearest to him.

—Marcel Proust

All for Love

If I ever really love it will be like Mary Queen of Scots, who said of her Bothwell that she could follow him around the world in her nightie.

—J. M. Barrie, *What Every Woman Knows*

Awakening

One can find women who have never had one love affair, but it is rare indeed to find any who have only had one.

—François, Duc de la Rochefoucauld

No Guaranty

No love can be bound by oath or covenant to secure it against a higher love.

—Ralph Waldo Emerson

Repute

A woman does not want her love affairs talked about. Yet she wants everybody to know that someone loves her.

—André Maurois

What Lips My Lips Have Kissed

What lips my lips have kissed, and where, and why,
I have forgotten, and what arms have lain
Under my head till morning; but the rain
Is full of ghosts tonight, that tap and sign
Upon the glass and listen for reply,
And in my heart there stirs a quiet pain
For unremembered lads that not again
Will turn to me at midnight with a cry.
Thus in the winter stands the lonely tree,
Nor knows what birds have vanished one by one,
Yet knows its boughs more silent than before:
I cannot say what loves have come and gone,
I only know that summer sang in me
A little while, that in me sings no more.

—Edna St. Vincent Millay

PANGS

Difficulté Vaincue

Next to being married, a girl likes to be crossed in love
a little now and then.

— Jane Austen, *Pride and Prejudice*

Growth

Every little girl knows about love. It is only her capac-
ity to suffer because of it that increases.

— Françoise Sagan

Remorse

At twenty she loved Z., at twenty-four she married N.,
not because she loved him, but because she thought
him a good, wise, ideal man. The couple lived happily;
everyone envies them, and indeed their life passes
smoothly and placidly; she is satisfied, and, when
people discuss love, she says that for family life not love
nor passion is wanted, but affection. But once the
music played suddenly, and, inside her heart, everything broke up like ice in spring: she remembered Z.

and her love for him, and she thought with despair that her life was ruined, spoilt forever, and that she was unhappy. Then it happened to her with the New Year greetings; when people wished her "New Happiness," she indeed longed for new happiness.

—Anton Chekhov, *Notebook*

Forlorn

We are never so defenseless against suffering as when we love, never so forlornly unhappy as when we have lost our love object or its love.

—Sigmund Freud

Afflicted

People who are not in love fail to understand how an intelligent man can suffer because of a very ordinary woman. This is like being surprised that anyone can be stricken with cholera because of a creature so insignificant as the common bacillus.

*   *   *

To think I have wasted years of my life, that I have longed for death, that the greatest love that I have ever known has been for a woman who did not please me, who was not my style.

—Marcel Proust

34

Exalted

"Let us not speak, for the love we bear one another—
  Let us hold hands and look."
She, such a very ordinary little woman;
  He, such a thumping crook;
But both, for a moment, little lower than the angels
  In the teashop's ingle-nook.

    —John Betjeman, *In a Bath Teashop*

Odi Et Amo

I hate her and I love her.
You ask, how can that be?
I don't know, but it's so
And I'm in agony.

    —Catullus

Pain

There is no pain equal to that which two lovers can
inflict on one another. . . . It is when we begin to hurt
those whom we love that the guilt with which we are
born becomes intolerable, and since all those whom
we love intensely and continuously grow part of us,
and as we hate ourselves in them, so we torture ourselves and them together.

    —Cyril Connolly

Gone

I sit at home
In our room
By our bed
Gazing at your pillow.

—Hitomaro, A.D. 700

Recovery

"It's better now . . . sometimes there are whole days when I only think of you now and then."

—J. T.

Jealousy

This evening I observed my wife mighty dull, and I myself was not mighty fond, because of some harsh words she did give me at noon, out of a jealousy at my being abroad this morning, which, God knows, it was upon the business of the office unexpectedly: but I to bed, not thinking but that she would come after me. But waking by and by out of a slumber, which I usually fall into presently after my coming into the bed, I found she did not prepare to come to bed, but got fresh candles, and more wood for her fire, it being mighty cold, too. At this being troubled, I after a while prayed her to come to bed; so after an hour or two, she silent,

gone

and I now and then praying her to come to bed, she fell out into a fury, that I was a rogue, and false to her. I did, as I might truly, deny it, and was mightily troubled, but all would not serve. At last, about one o'clock, she came to my side of the bed, and drew my curtains open, and with the tongs red hot at the end made as if she did design to pinch me with them: at which, in dismay, I rose up, and with a few words she laid them down, and did by little and little, very sillyly, let all the discourse fall; and about two, but with much seeming difficulty, came to bed, and there lay well all night, and long in bed talking together with much pleasure, it being, I know, nothing but her doubt of my going out yesterday without telling her of my going, which did vex her, poor wretch! last night; and I cannot blame her jealousy, though it do vex me to the heart.

—Samuel Pepys

SEDUCTION

Invitation

A woman will sometimes forgive the man who tries to seduce her, said Talleyrand, but never the man who misses an opportunity when offered.

Siege

Love is a besieger with allies inside the castle.*

Hope

When the denial comes fainter and fainter,
And her eyes give what her tongue does deny,
Ah what a trembling I feel when I venture,
Ah what a trembling does usher my joy!

—From *An Evening's Love*, John Dryden

*Adapted from various sources; also, "A fortress that parleys is half taken."

Promises

Lovers' vows do not reach the ears of the gods.

—Callimachus, third century B.C.

Roving

Licence my roving hands, and let them go
Before, behind, between, above, below.
O my America, my new found land,
My kingdom, safeliest when with one man manned.

—John Donne

Reinforcement

I achieved my best results, however, by attacking novices—whose moral principles and prejudices hindered the carrying-out of my intentions—in the company of another woman. I learned already in my early youth that young girls are difficult to seduce because they lack the courage, whereas in the company of a friend they easily surrender: the weakness of one excuses the fall of the other.

—Giovanni Casanova, *Memoirs*

Courtly Ways

I

A good lover will behave just as elegantly at dawn as at any other time. He drags himself out of bed with a look of dismay on his face. The lady urges him on: "Come, my friend, it's getting light. You don't want anyone to find you here." He gives a heart-felt sign, as if to say that the night has not been nearly long enough and that it is agony to leave. When he is up, he does not immediately start putting on his trousers. Instead he approaches the lady and whispers to her what remains to be said from their night's exchanges. Though in fact he is doing nothing at the moment, he vaguely pretends to be fastening his sash.

Presently he raises the lattice and the two lovers go and stand by the side door. He tells her how he dreads the coming day, which will keep them apart. Then almost imperceptibly he glides away. The lady watches him go, and this moment of parting will remain among her most charming memories.

II

He is wearing loose violet trousers, an orange hunting-costume, so lightly coloured that one can hardly tell whether it has been dyed or not, a white robe of stiff silk and a glossy robe of beaten silk. His clothes, which have been thoroughly moistened by the dew, hang loosely about him. From the dishevelment of his side locks one can tell how negligently he must have tucked his hair into his black lacquered headdress when he got up. He wants to return and write his next-morning letter before the dew on the morning-glories has had time to vanish. . . .

As he walks along, he passes a house with an open lattice. He is on his way to report for official duty, but he cannot help stopping to raise the blind slightly and peep into the room. It amuses him to think that some other man has probably been spending the night here and has recently got up and left, just as he himself has done.

—Sei Shonagon, *Pillow Book*

Where

Seduction is best pursued in gardens and cemeteries, under a tree, on a boat, and in front of the fire.

—J. T.

Faint Heart

"Of all forms of caution," wrote Bertrand Russell, "caution in love is perhaps the most fatal to true happiness."

Passage

L'amore fa passare il tempo;
Il tempo fa passare l'amore.*

—Italian proverb

Expedition

When we go out on a love-making expedition, we light
our fire; we take our lime gourd (and chew betel-nut),
we take our tobacco (and smoke it). Food we do not
take, we would be ashamed to do so. We walk, we
arrive at a large tree, we sit down, we search each
other's heads and consume the lice, we tell the woman
that we want to copulate. After it is over we return
to the village. In the village we go to the bachelors'
house, lie down, and chatter. When we are alone he
takes off the pubic leaf, she takes off her fiber skirt: we
go to sleep.

—B. Malinowski, *The Sexual Life
of Savages in Northwestern Melanesia*,
cited in Morton M. Hunt,
The Natural History of Love

*"Love makes the time pass;
Time makes love pass."

43

Love in Russia Today—Two Traditional Jokes

I
Students

In the amphitheater of the lecture hall a note is passed down several rows to a brown-haired girl, who unfolds it. The note says, "I like your looks. Want to screw?"

The girl turns around and spots a boy several rows back waving shyly.

She nods and sends back a note saying, "Your hint received and understood. Meet me behind the gymnasium at eight o'clock tonight."

II
Official Life

Minister Ivanov's wife knows he has a mistress but doesn't know who. Consumed by curiosity, she badgers him until he admits that she is a dancer in the Kirov Ballet. Finally they both attend a performance in honor of a visiting delegation. From their box she peers at the dancers through her opera glass until she spots a likely candidate. "The one on the right in the second row?" she asks.

"No," said Ivanov, "she's Petrov's—the Minister of Light Industry."

"How about the tall one in the middle . . . with the bony legs?"

"She's Admiral Semyonoff's."

His wife goes on studying. "I have it! The second from the right in front!"

The Minister nods. His wife puts down the opera glass and smiles complacently. "*Our* mistress is prettier than *their* mistress," she announces with satisfaction.

Communication

I have made love to ten thousand women since I was thirteen and a half. It wasn't in any way a vice. I've no sexual vices. But I needed to communicate.

> —Georges Simenon, in an interview
> with Federico Fellini in *L'Express*.
> (His wife claimed there were only 1,500
> or so—mostly tarts, of course.)

Rx

The medical advantages of frequent intercourse with several different women were constantly emphasized in Taoist and yin-yang literature. "Those who can exercise the sexual act scores of times in one day *sine umquam semen emittendo* will thereby cure all their ills and live to a great age. If the act is performed with a number of different women, its benefit will increase. It is best to engage in the sexual act with ten or more different women on one night." Similar prescriptions are found in works of the T'ang dynasty and later.

> —Ivan Morris, *The World of the Shining Prince*

FULFILLMENT

Summation

Love and work . . . work and love, that's all there is.*

—Sigmund Freud

Vitalized

. . . when a man and woman are successfully in love, their whole activity is energized and victorious. They walk better, their digestion improves, they think more clearly, their secret worries drop away, the world is fresh and interesting, and they can do more than they dreamed that they could do. In love of this kind sexual intimacy is not the dead end of desire as it is in romantic or promiscuous love, but periodic affirmation of the inward delight of desire pervading an active life. Love of this sort can grow: it is not, like youth itself, a moment that comes and is gone and remains only a memory of something which cannot be recovered. It can grow because it has something to grow upon and to grow with; it is not contracted and stale because it

*Vide Kahlil Gibran, "Work is love made visible."

has for its object, not the mere relief of physical tension, but all the objects with which the two lovers are concerned. They desire their worlds in each other, and therefore their love is as interesting as their worlds and their worlds are as interesting as their love.

—Walter Lippmann

Response

To love is to enjoy seeing, touching, and sensing with all the senses, as closely as possible, a lovable object which loves in return.

—Stendhal, *De l'Amour*

Icon

[In wise love] each defines the secret self of the other, and refusing to believe in the mere daily self, creates a mirror where the lover or the beloved sees an image to copy in daily life; for love also creates the Mask.

—William Butler Yeats

More Blessed

There is less joy in being loved than in loving.

—J. T.

Oasis

Many people when they fall in love look for a little haven of refuge from the world, where they can be sure of being admired when they are not admirable, and praised when they are not praiseworthy.

—Bertrand Russell

Bertrand Russell

Now I will make up an exact statement, and please keep it in mind however dumb I may be, because it is at all times true.

1. I want to keep you and I want not to ruin your life. . . . Compared to these two, all other things in life are trivial to me. Don't doubt this.

2. I want to accomplish, during my life, a good deal more work in philosophy. . . .

3. I want to write general things on religion and morals and popular philosophy. I could do this even if I were discredited, because I could publish anonymously.

4. I like teaching, but that is inessential.

I have put these four in order of importance, the most important first. . . . Whatever may be involved in our holding to each other, the harm to me will be less than if we parted. I believe seriously that the spring of life would be broken in me if we parted. . . . If I have you, there are other goods that may be added; if I don't have you, there are no other goods. . . . I have never imagined such love. I have had the feeling too that I ought to keep it back from you so as not to interfere with your freedom—but I can't. . . . With you there is life and joy and peace and all good things—away from you there is turmoil and anguish and blank despair.

—Letter to Lady Ottoline Morrell*

Parallel

Love does not consist in gazing at each other but in looking together in the same direction.

—Antoine de Saint-Exupéry

Accompaniment

Love is not the dying moan of a distant violin—it's the triumphant twang of a bedspring.

—S. J. Perelman

*Among over two thousand. His memoirs describe some days with her that "remain in my memory as among the few moments when life seemed all that it might be, but hardly ever is."

Gift

I gave what other women gave
That stepped out of their clothes,
But when this soul, its body off,
Naked to naked goes,
He it has found shall find therein
What none other knows.

—William Butler Yeats

COURTSHIP

Intentions

The hardest task of a girl's life is to prove to a man that his intentions are serious.

—Helen Rowland

Wisdom

In understanding the emotions, men, compared to women, are children.

—J.T.

Fated

Marie-Sygne Claudel, on her engagement to Christopher Northbourne: "When I saw that his family motto was '*J'ayme à jamais*'* I knew I was lost. What could I do? I had to marry him."

*"I love forever."

Eloping

Dame Olave, a daughter and coheir of Sir Henry Sharington of Lacock being in love with John Talbot ... and her father not consenting that she should marry him: discoursing with him one night from the battlements of the Abbey Church; said she, "I will leap down to you": her sweetheart replied, he would catch her then: but he did not believe she would have done it: she leapt down and did something break the fall: Mr. Talbot caught her in his arms, but she struck him dead.

—John Aubrey, *Brief Lives*

Once-Over

Sir William Roper ... came one morning pretty early to my Lord, with a proposal to marry one of his daughters. My Lord's daughters were then both together abed in a trucklebed in their father's chamber asleep. He carries Sir William into the chamber and takes the sheet by the corner and suddenly whips it off. They lay on their backs, and their smocks up as high as their arm-pits. This awakened them, and immediately they turned on their bellies. Quoth Roper, I have seen both sides, and so gave a pat on the buttock he made choice of, saying, "Thou art mine."

—John Aubrey, *Brief Lives*

Marry

I feel sad when I don't see you. Be married, why won't you? And come to live with me. I will make you as happy as I can. You shall not be obliged to work hard; and when you are tired, you may lie in my lap and I will sing you to rest.... I will play you a tune upon the violin as often as you ask and as well as I can; and leave off smoking, if you say so.... I will always be very kind to you, I think, because I love you so well. I will not make you bring in wood and water, or feed the pig, or milk the cow, or go to the neighbors to borrow milk. Will you be married?

—Nineteenth-century American love letter

Introduction

On Sunday, December 6, 1992, PBS viewers were startled by Dick Cavett's description of Harpo Marx's presentation to Tallulah Bankhead at a posh gathering. Harpo, a determined womanizer, was at best a rough diamond; Tallulah, a feline actress, was the daughter of a Speaker of the House and the niece of a Senator. It was impressed on Harpo that he should be on his best behavior. The encounter began auspiciously enough.

HARPO: Good evening, Miss Bankhead.
TALLULAH: Good evening, Mr. Marx.
Then things gave way a bit.
HARPO: Miss Bankhead, I want to fuck you.
TALLULAH: And so you shall, you little rascal!

Mark Twain in Love

On board ship on an expedition to the Holy Land, Clemens made the acquaintance of Charles J. Langdon, a young man from Elmira, New York, who was a great admirer of his. At some point, Langdon showed him a miniature of his sister Olivia. Clemens could not forget her face and resolved to meet her. He later maneuvered an invitation to visit the Langdon home for a week, and in that week he fell thoroughly for Livy, as the family called her. On the last day of his visit he said to Langdon, "Charley, my week is up, and I must go home." Langdon did not press him to stay longer, but he said, "We'll have to stand it I guess, but you mustn't leave before tonight."

"I ought to go by the first train," said Clemens gloomily. "I am in love."

"In what?"

"In love—with your sister and I ought to get away from here."

Langdon was now genuinely alarmed: no one was good enough for his sister, the family's darling.

"Look here, Clemens," he said, "there's a train in half an hour. I'll help you catch it. Don't wait 'til tonight. Go now."

—*Faber Book of Anecdotes*

MARRIAGE

The Duchess of Marlborough describes how her husband came home from the wars and with soldierly dispatch "pleasured me in his boots."

A Good Wife

The man must look after the things that go on outside the home. A husband therefore has to travel about in rain, wind, snow, and hail; now drenched, now parched, now sweating, now shivering, ill-fed, ill-lodged, ill-warmed, and ill-bedded. But he is sustained by the thought of the care his wife will take of him on his return, and of the ease, the joys, and the pleasures which she will give him, or have done for him in her presence: to have his boots taken off before a good fire, to have his feet washed and fresh shoes and hose put on, to be offered good food and drink, to be well served and well looked after, well bedded in white sheets and nightcaps, well covered with good furs, and comforted with other intimate joys, loves, and secrets whereof I am silent.

—From a Medieval Marriage Guide (paraphrased J. T.)

Second Marriages

The triumph of hope over experience.

—Samuel Johnson

Start

Love set you going like a fat gold watch.
The midwife slapped your footsoles, and your bald cry
Took its place among the elements.

—Sylvia Plath

Conjugal Love

It is a deep unity maintained by the will and deliber-
ately strengthened by habit; reinforced by (in Chris-
tian marriages) the grace, which both parents ask, and
receive, from God. They can have this love for each
other even at those moments when they do not like
each other; as you love yourself even when you do not
like yourself. They can retain this love, even when each
would easily, if they allowed themselves, be "in love"
with someone else. "Being in love" first moved them
to promise fidelity: this quieter love enables them to
keep the promise. It is on this love that the engine of
marriage is run; being in love was the explosion that
started it.

—C. S. Lewis

Support

The tragedy of modern marriage is that married couples no longer enjoy the support of society, although marriage, difficult enough at any time, requires social sanction. Thus, in the past, married women censured the unmarried; the constant punished the inconstant; society outlawed the divorced and the dwellers-in-sin. Now it does the opposite.

—Cyril Connolly

Eclipsed

*Tu m'as rendu fades tous les hommes, et médiocres tous les destins.**

—de Montherlant

*"For me you have rendered all other men dull, and all other lives uninteresting" (J.T. paraphrase). John Julius Norwich observes that this "must be the most perfect compliment that any woman could pay her husband."

The Long Murmur I

Marriage is a fifty-year chat. Like physical love, talk is not a detached event, but flows from the overall chemistry. When my daughters are interested in a boy, I sometimes ask, "Do you just babble a lot?"

One of the girls turned serious at the question and shook her head. I was not surprised when the attachment was broken off.

—J. T.

The Long Murmur II

Every summer for as far back as I could remember, I had watched Robert and Mary Jones walking down the beach to the water for a swim. They would walk at a leisurely pace, several feet apart, conversing. I never overheard much of what they said, but it was apparent that the conversation ranged from serious discussion to banter. Often it was punctuated with laughter; I remember the laughter most vividly. When they reached the water, they would wade in, still talking, losing their balance somewhat on the rocks underfoot, talk some more, and, finally, sink in and swim around a little—in a semi-upright position that allowed them to continue talking. Their enjoyment of each other was arresting—sharp as pepper, golden. I have seen other happy old couples, but this picture of the Joneses, renewed many times, came to represent to me an essence of human exchange—something indescribably moving and precious, which comes to fruition only toward the end of a lifelong marriage.

—*The New Yorker*, "Talk of the Town," August 30, 1976

Friendship I

A good marriage is based on a talent for friendship.

—Friedrich Nietzsche

Friendship II

Love is blind; friendship closes its eyes.*

—Lord Byron

Whom God Hath Joined

The only difference about being married is that you don't have to get out of bed to fart.

—Jimmy Goldsmith

*"Love draws a veil over all transgressions." Proverbs 10:12.

Help Wanted

I have found it impossible to carry the heavy burden of responsibility and to discharge my duties as King as I would wish to do without the help and support of the woman I love.

—Edward VIII's abdication speech

De Profundis

Dear Alf, I seen you last night in my dream. O my dear I cried at waking up. What a silly girl you been and got. The pain is bad this morning but I laugh at the sollum clocks of the sisters and the sawbones. I can see they think I am booked but they don't know what has befalen between you and me. How could I die and leave you Dear. I spill my medicin this morning thinking of my Dear. Hopeing this finds you well no more now from yours truly Liz.*

—Cited in *Love*, by Walter de la Mare

*The writer of the letter died a few days later.

FIDELITY

Whither Thou Goest

And Ruth said, "Intreat me not to leave thee, or to return from following after thee: for whither thou goest, I will go; and where thou lodgest, I will lodge: thy people shall be my people, and thy God my God:
   "Where thou diest, will I die, and there will I be buried: the Lord do so to me, and more also, if aught but death part thee and me."

—Ruth 1:16–17

Be True

Ah, love, let us be true
To one another! for the world, which seems
To lie before us like a land of dreams,
So various, so beautiful, so new,
Hath really neither joy, nor love, nor light,
Nor certitude, nor peace, nor help for pain;
And we are here as on a darkling plain
Swept with confused alarms of struggle and flight,
Where ignorant armies clash by night.

—Matthew Arnold, *Dover Beach*

Change I

We are not the same persons this year as last; nor are those we love. It is a happy chance if we, changing, continue to love a changed person.

—Somerset Maugham

Change II

Let me not to the marriage of true minds
Admit impediments. Love is not love
Which alters when it alteration finds.
Or bends with the remover to remove:
O no! It is an ever-fixed mark
That looks on tempests, and is never shaken;
It is the star to every wandering bark,
Whose worth's unknown, although his height
  be taken.
Love's not Time's fool, though rosy lips and cheeks
Within his bending sickle's compass come;
Love alters not with his brief hours and weeks,
But bears it out even to the edge of doom.
  If this be error, and upon me prov'd,
  I never writ, nor no man ever lov'd.

—William Shakespeare, *Sonnets*, 116

The River Merchant's Wife

At fourteen I married My Lord you.
I never laughed, being bashful.
Lowering my head, I looked at the wall.
Called to, a thousand times, I never looked back.

At fifteen I stopped scowling,
I desired my dust to be mingled with yours
For ever and for ever and for ever.

At sixteen you departed,
You went into far Ku-to-yen,
   by the river of swirling eddies,
And you have been gone five months.
The monkeys make sorrowful noise overhead.

I grow older.
If you are coming down through the narrows of
   the river Kiang
Please let me know beforehand,
And I will come out to meet you
As far as Cho-fu-Sa.

                    —Rihaku, trans. Ezra Pound (abridged J.T.)

Fate

When I lose you I might as well be dead. There will be no comfort left, when you have met your doom—nothing but grief.

—Andromache to Hector in Homer's *Iliad*

Parce que c'était lui

Asked about his deep and rich attachment to Étienne de la Boetie, Montaigne gave the wonderful answer: "Because it was him; because it was me."

INFIDELITY

Support

The chain of marriage is so heavy that it takes two to bear it; sometimes three.

—Alexandre Dumas *fils*

Bonanza

The first thrill of adultery is entering the house. Everything there has been paid for by the other man.

—John Updike

Vacancy

The man who marries his mistress creates a vacancy in the position.*

—Jimmy Goldsmith

*Slightly rephrased by J.T. Also, of course, the woman who marries her lover, the ultimate in this maneuver being Jane Digby Ellenborough Venningen Theotoky El Mesrab—"to name only her legal attachments"—as Lesley Blanch says of her in *The Wilder Shores of Love*.

Deb

Samuel Pepys and his wife had fearful battles over his infatuation with her maid, Deb. Finally poor Deb got the sack. Then Pepys tracked her home and started in all over again. Renewed wars with Mrs. P. Finally Pepys contracted in writing to steer clear of Deb forever. His diary records him as:

> most absolutely resolved, if ever I can master this bout, never to give her [his wife] occasion while I live of more trouble of this or any other kind. . . . Did this night begin to pray to God upon my knees alone in my chamber, which God knows I cannot yet do heartily.

Clues

Later she wondered how she could have been so blind, and blind so long. The signs were abundant: the sand, his eccentric comings and goings, his giving up smoking, his triumphant exuberance whenever Sally was at the same party, the tender wifely touch (this glimpse had stung at the time, to endure in Ruth's memory) with which Sally on one occasion had picked up Jerry's wrist, inviting him to dance.

—John Updike

A Symmetry

Woman wants monogamy;
Man delights in novelty.
Love is woman's moon and sun;
Man has other forms of fun.

Woman lives but in her lord;
Count to ten, and man is bored.*
With this the gist and sum of it,
What earthly good can come of it?

—Dorothy Parker, *Not So Deep as a Well*

Family Friend

Ninon de Lenclos was the mistress of the Marquis de
Sévigné, later of his son, and perhaps, we are given to
believe, of his grandson. She died at the age of eighty-
five, and I have read that an obituary described her as
"renowned for her chastity in the last years of her life."

---

*Vide Byron: "Man's love is of man's life a thing apart. 'Tis
woman's whole existence."

Courtly Love

In a famous case, a knight sued in the Court of Love to require that his lady accept him in her bed. She had formerly had a lover, but had promised the knight her favors if anything changed. Then her husband died, and she married the lover. So the knight applied for the job.

Queen Adele determined that between husband and wife there are many ties, but not love. Therefore, the lady now had no lover, and her promise to the knight must be honored.

DISILLUSIONMENT

Gauge

We perceive when love begins and when it declines by our embarrassment when alone together.

—Jean de la Bruyère

Autopsy

Whenever a husband and wife begin to discuss their marriage, they are giving evidence at an inquest.

—Elbert Hubbard

Fatigue

Nothing ages a man like living always with the same woman.

—Norman Douglas

Calm

A man can be happy with any woman as long as he does not love her.

—Oscar Wilde

Enragée

Discrimination

Love consists in overestimating the difference between one woman and another.*

—George Bernard Shaw

Enragée

There is no fury like an ex-wife searching for a new lover.

—Cyril Connolly

Disadvantages

The pleasure is fleeting, the position ridiculous,† and the expense prohibitive.

—Earl of Chesterfield

*Vide H. L. Mencken, "Love is the delusion that one woman differs from another."

†And Chesterfield had not even undergone the contortions of sex in the back seat.

Blind

Love often blinds reason, and usually precipitates those who follow him into a gulf of misfortunes, then, taking flight, leaves them to extricate themselves as they are able.

—Elizabeth I

Reheating

It is like a cigar. If it goes out, you can light it again but it never tastes quite the same.*

—Field Marshal Wavell

Extrapolation

Many a man in love with a dimple makes the mistake of marrying the whole girl.

—Stephen Leacock

Vide Bertolt Brecht, "Love is also like a coconut which is good while it is fresh, but you have to spit it out when the juice is gone, what's left tastes bitter."

Carefree

I think of the days
Before I met her
When I seemed to have
No troubles at all.

—Fujiwara No Atsutada, tenth century A.D.

Dispensables

Four be the things I'd be better without:
Love, curiosity, freckles and doubt.

*   *   *

Oh, life is a glorious cycle of song,
A medley of extemporanea;
And love is a thing that can never go wrong;
And I am Marie of Roumania.

—Dorothy Parker

Anguish

May those who are born after me
Never travel such roads of love.

—Hitomaro, A.D. 700

MYSTERY

Wonders

There be three things which are too wonderful for me, yea, four which I know not:
The way of an eagle in the air; the way of a serpent upon a rock; the way of a ship in the midst of the sea; and the way of a man with a maid.

—Proverbs 30:18–19

Mystère

I have never conceived of love without mystery, and where there was mystery there for me has already been love.

—Charles-Augustin Sainte-Beuve

Gilding

Love: The veils of purple and gold that youth drapes over the nudity of life.

—Johann von Goethe

Unveiling

As we make sex less secretive, we may rob it of its power to hold men and women together.

—Thomas Szasz

Understanding

Husbands rarely understand their wives; wives usually understand their husbands all too well.

—J. T.

Renunciation

I here and now, finally and forever, give up knowing anything about love, or wanting to know. I believe it doesn't exist, save as a word: a sort of wailing phoenix that is really the wind in the trees.

—D. H. Lawrence

HOLY LOVE

Difference

Liszt said to me today that God alone deserves to be
loved. It may be true, but when one has loved a man it
is very different to love God.

—Georges Sand

Teacher

Amor magnus doctor est.*

—Saint Augustine

Guide

The astrolabe of the mysteries of God is love.

—Jalaluddin Rumi

*"Love is a great teacher."

Hierarchy

Angels, I read, belong to nine different orders. Seraphs are the highest; they are aflame with love for God, and stand closer to him than the others. Seraphs love God; cherubs, who are second, possess perfect knowledge of him. So love is greater than knowledge; how could I have forgotten?

—Annie Dillard

Illumination

All, everything that I understand, I understand only because I love.

—Leo Tolstoy, *War and Peace*

As You Will

Ama et quod vis fac.*

—Saint Augustine

*"Love, and do as you will." That is, if you truly love your wife or your neighbor, rules are not needed.

INDEX